Mr. Mumble

story and paintings by

PETER CATALANOTTO

ORCHARD BOOKS   NEW YORK

To DJ...he knows why.

Remember, no man is a failure who has friends
_____

Copyright © 1990 by Peter Catalanotto
First Orchard Paperbacks edition 1994

Orchard Books
95 Madison Avenue, New York, NY 10016

Manufactured in the United States of America.
Printed by Barton Press, Inc. Bound by Horowitz/Rae.
Book design by Mina Greenstein
The text of this book is set in 18 pt. ITC Zapf International Medium. The
illustrations are watercolor paintings reproduced in full color.
Hardcover   2   4   6   8   10   9   7   5   3
Paperback   2   4   6   8   10   9   7   5   3   1

Library of Congress Cataloging-in-Publication Data
Catalanotto, Peter.
Mr. Mumble / Peter Catalanotto.
p.   cm. "A Richard Jackson book"—Half t.p. Summary: When Mr.
Mumble gets a bird in his throat, no one can understand him.
ISBN 0-531-05880-8 (tr.)   ISBN 0-531-08480-9 (lib. bdg.)
ISBN 0-531-07052-2 (pbk.)
[1. Humorous stories.]   I. Title.   PZ7.C26878Mr   1991
[E]—dc20   89-48940

Saturday morning,
Mr. Mumby awoke with a tickle (*cough, cough*)
in his throat.

"I hope I'm not (*cough*) coming down
with something," he said to himself,
"for I have so much (*cough*) to do today!"

Shopping
Bakery - Bagels
Fruit Stand - Pears
Grocery - Stew
Tailor - coat
5&10 - clock

As he was getting dressed
the phone rang.

(*cough, cough*)
"Hello, Mumby speaking," he said.

"Mr. Mumble?" inquired the operator.
"I'm sorry to have bothered you, Mr. Mumble.
I was calling a Mr. Mumby."

She hung up.

"But I am Mr. Mumby," he said to himself.
"Oh well."

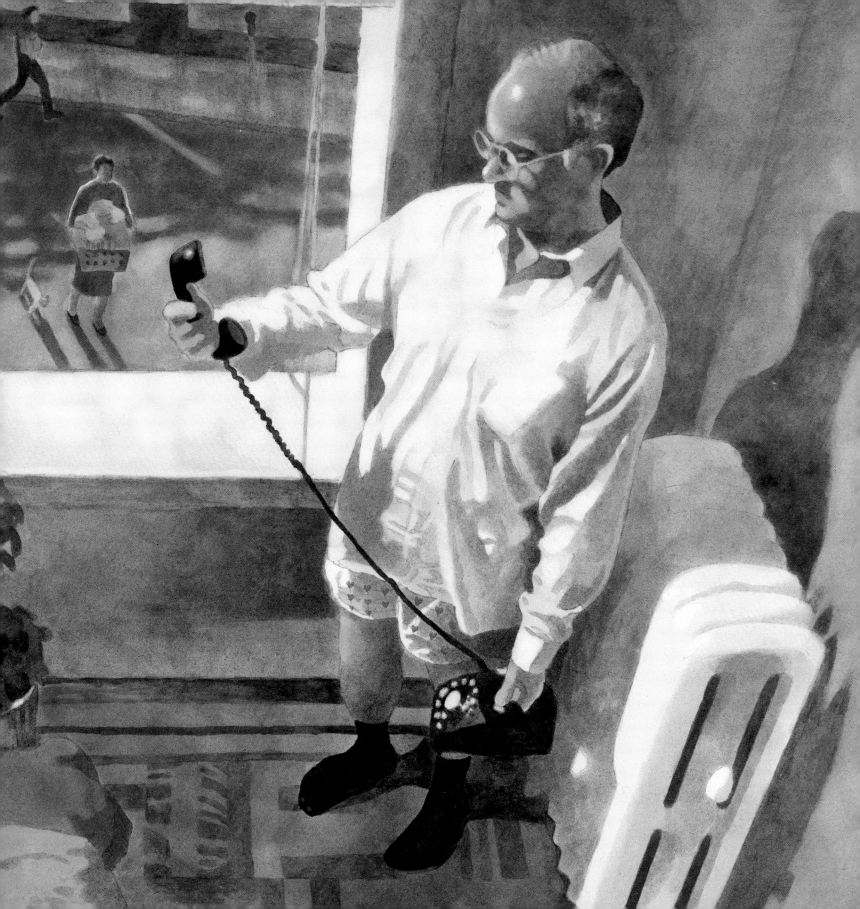

On his way to breakfast,
Mr. Mumby passed his landlady
carrying
a huge basket of laundry.
She heard Mr. Mumby say:
"May I marry your (*cough*) cat?"

"Certainly not!" the landlady replied
and hurried into her apartment.

[What Mr. Mumby really asked was:
"May I help carry (*cough*) that?"]

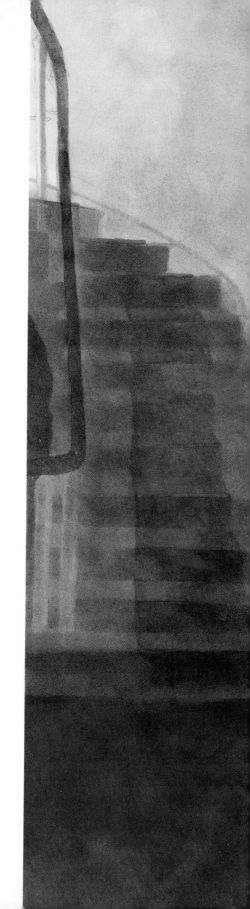

At the diner,
he was served two scarecrow legs
and a car muffler.
Mr. Mumby smiled (*cough, cough*) politely,
paid his bill, and left the restaurant.

[What he really ordered was
two scrambled eggs and a corn muffin.]

At the bakery,
he was handed a dozing beagle.

[Mr. Mumby had asked (*cough*)
for a dozen (*cough*) bagels.]

And imagine his bewilderment
when at the fruit stand
he asked the woman for a
(*cough, cough*)
pound of pears…

...and then the grocer (*cough*)
for a can of stew.

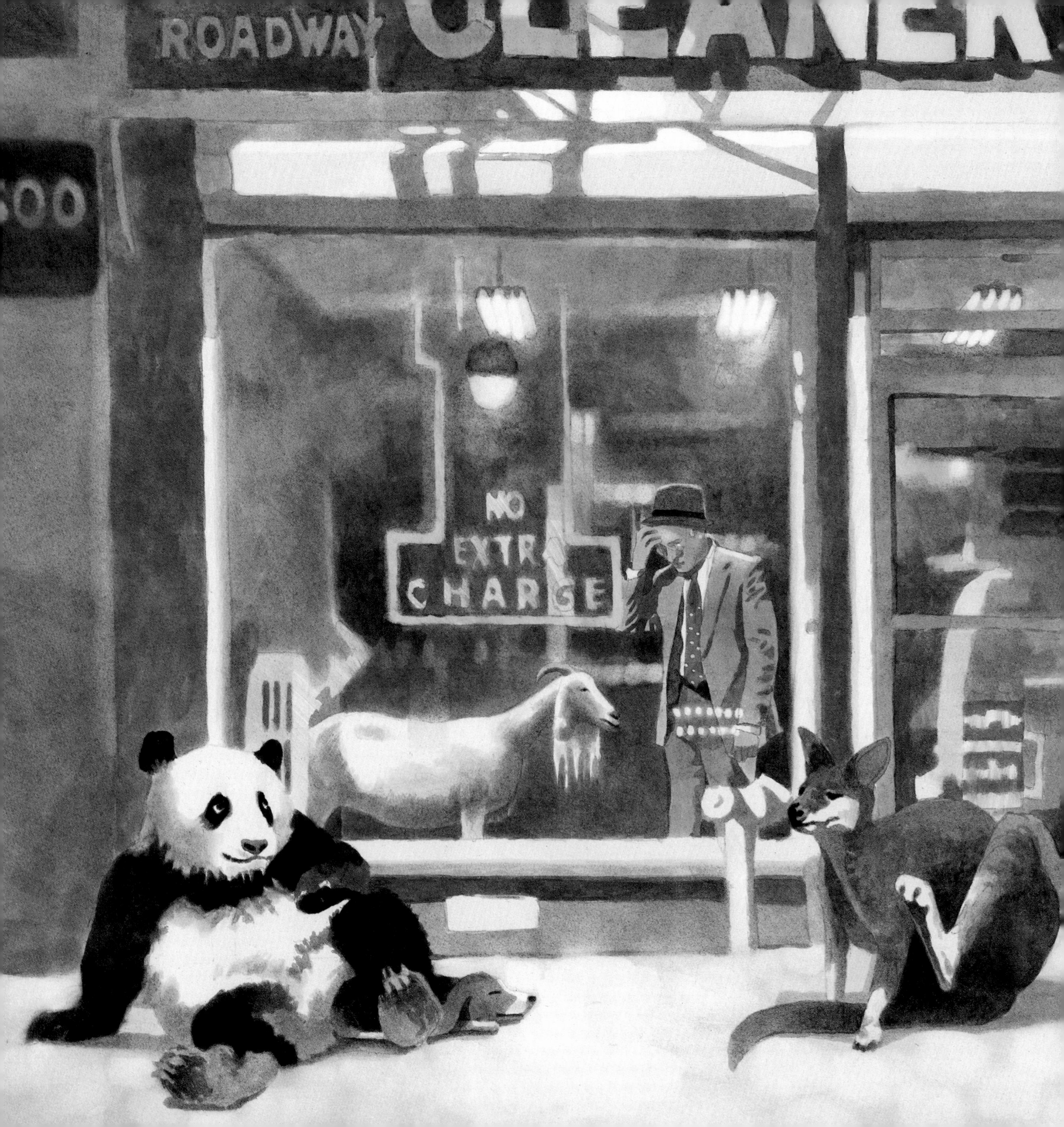
ROADWAY
NO
EXTR
CHARGE

Next, at the tailor's,
he was sure he'd mentioned (*cough*)
only his light tan coat.

"Oh my!"
coughed poor Mr. Mumby.

Then at the five-and-dime
a clerk gave him
an aardvark
when he asked for
an alarm (*cough*) clock…

...and the haberdasher
handed him a muskrat
when all he'd said to the man
was he needed (*cough*)
a new hat....

At last
Mr. Mumby bleated as best he could:
"No one
seems to under(*cough*)stand me today!"

He thought he'd better see a doctor.

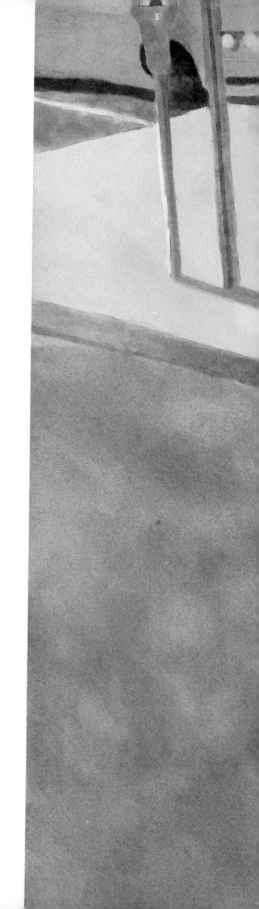

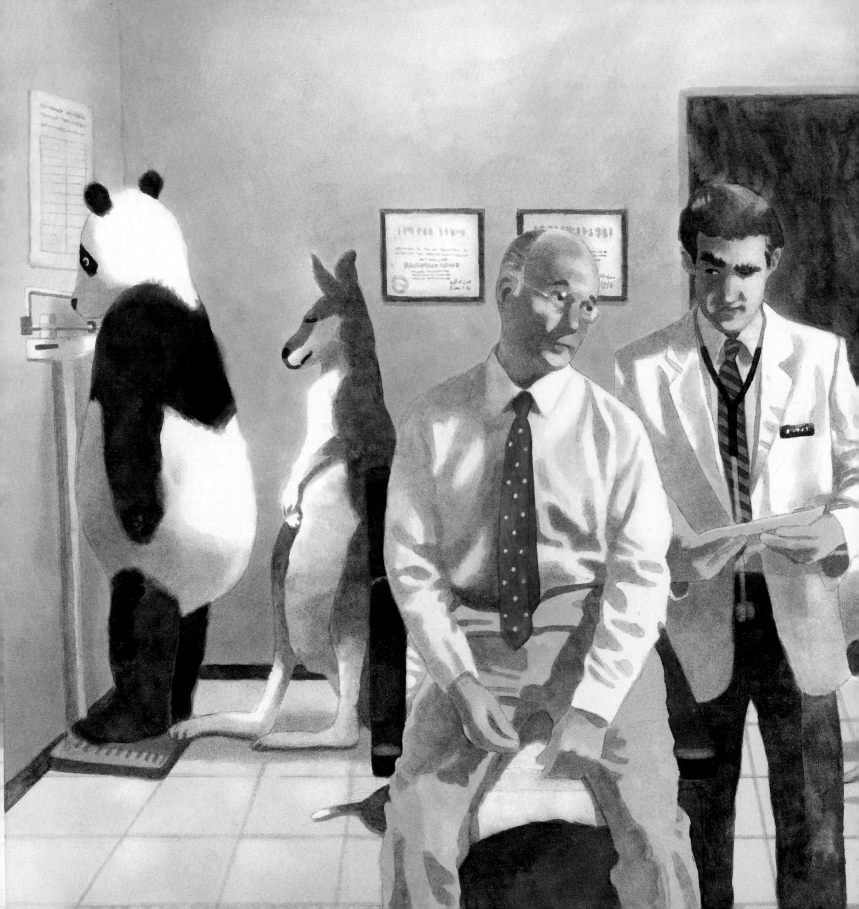

When
the doctor
asked Mr. Mumby
to open wide and say
"Ahhhh…"

...finally...

...everyone understood the problem.
(*squawk!*)

Smiling at last, Mr. Mumby added another shop to his list.
The pet store.
"I wonder," he said, quite clearly now, "what an aardvark eats."